Cooking in the Nude

Playful Gourmets

Designed by Carolyn Weary Brandt
Edited by Katherine A. Neale and Keri D. Moser

First published in 1987 by Wellton Books.

Library of Congress Catalog Card Number 96-75273
ISBN 0-943231-97-3

Printed in Canada
Published by Howell Press, Inc., 1713-2D Allied Lane,
Charlottesville, Virginia 22903.
Telephone: (804) 977-4006
www.howellpress.com

Third Printing 2000

HOWELL PRESS

TABLE OF CONTENTS

INTRODUCTION

*C*aution: This book is intended for lovers and potential lovers! Excessive use of our romantic recipes may result in loss of sleep. We suggest you reserve these menus for only your most special and playful occasions.

Remember that attitude and ambiance are primary ingredients of seductive dining. Be sure you understand the importance of "Before Play" and the risk of "Cheap Frills" before you try the first recipe!

To enjoy each dining experience to its fullest, approach every recipe as the beginning of a new and uniquely exciting evening of seduction. Take the time to entice your companion with an "Appeteaser" before you offer the "Pièce de No Resistance." We've provided specific menu recommendations for each entrée, but you'll note that we never make mention of desserts. How you conclude each evening of dining is left totally to your imagination.

CHEAP FRILLS
(Creating the Mood)

*C*reating an atmosphere of intimacy and intrigue will captivate your intended lover before the first course is even served. The tactics that you employ will depend on your personality and intentions. Is your heart's desire a new acquaintance, your spouse, or something in between? If your companion is familiar with your environment and style of dining, creating the mood may involve a change in both. If the relationship is already intimate, what would you do differently if this were the evening of first seduction? Get the picture? Sure you do! Set the mood to realize your fantasy.

It doesn't take that much effort to put a tablecloth on the table, accent your setting with fresh flowers, and lower the lighting. A dimmer switch is a great cheap frill!

Your next step should be an exercise in self-expression. Table linens reflect your mood and can provide a very subtle, yet unmistakable, suggestion to your companion. Start with a solid color tablecloth. For variety, buy several sets of napkins. Choose the patterns that best express your playful personality. For example, an amorous and sultry tropical print in deliciously deep, rich colors conveys an aura of clandestine intrigue; a sporty, adventurous print in bright, vivid, spirited colors and patterns will portray you as bold and confident.

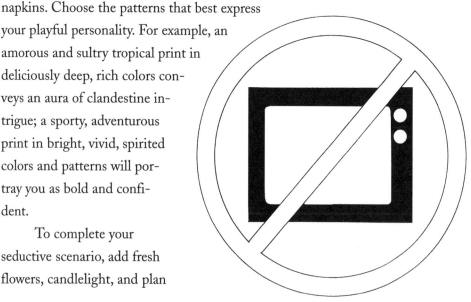

To complete your seductive scenario, add fresh flowers, candlelight, and plan your selection of music for the evening (television is counterproductive to seduction). Don't forget the obvious; turn on the answering machine, make babysitting arrangements for the kids (if you have any), and tell your best friend you're out of town.

You've paid attention to every delectable detail in creating the mood. The ambiance is perfect and you still have an hour before the object of your affection will be served the first course. You can relax now, take a deep breath, and reflect on the romantic rewards you're soon to reap.

DOES SIZE REALLY MATTER?
(Presentation)

*T*his question probably has been debated since Adam first cooked for Eve. Size most definitely matters when it comes to an appropriate selection of serving pieces and stemware. Au gratin dishes are recommended for many of our recipes. The 9" size is superb for entrées, while the 5" size is perfect for something on the side. An assortment of ramekins, pedestal dessert dishes, or small bowls is also a must for proper presentation of individual sauces, dressings, and condiments. Now we're not suggesting you throw away your everyday dishes or pull the china out of the closet—just add some variety to what you usually use and keep the mayonnaise jar off the table.

BEFORE PLAY
(Pantry Needs)

*Y*our pantry must become the foundation for adventurous dining endeavors. Each recipe that follows will include its own suggestions for seasonings and garnishes. Unless otherwise noted, the herbs and spices indicated in the recipes are dried. Tailor them to your tastes and experiment. Do not be afraid to take culinary license. Explore all the possibilities and give in to whimsy! (Nothing ventured, nothing gained!) A well-stocked pantry, including the following seasonings, spices, and garnishes, will allow you to prepare all our recipes.

♥ ♥ ♥ ♥ ♥ ♥ ♥ ♥ ♥ ♥ ♥ ♥ ♥ ♥ ♥ ♥

Dried Herbs and Spices:
Allspice
Basil
Bay leaves
Cayenne
Chervil
Cinnamon
Curry powder
Dill
Fines herbes
Garlic powder
Garlic salt
Ginger
Marjoram
Mustard, dry
Mustard seeds
Nutmeg
Onion powder
Oregano
Paprika
Peppercorns
Rosemary
Sage
Salt
Tarragon
Thyme
White pepper

Produce:
Basil
Chives
Dill
Garlic
Ginger root
Jalapeños
Lemons
Limes
Onions
Parsley
Rosemary
Thyme

Condiments and Staples:
Almonds, slivered
Artichoke hearts, marinated
Artichoke hearts, water-packed
Brown sugar
Capers
Cashews
Chilies, canned diced
Chow mein noodles, crispy
Chutney, fig, currant, and walnut
Cornstarch
Flour, all-purpose

Honey
Liquid smoke
Mustard, Dijon
Mustard, hot
Mustard, prepared
Olive oil
Oyster sauce (available in oriental markets)
Peanuts
Pecans
Pine nuts
Pistachios
Soy sauce
Sugar
Tabasco
Tarragon vinegar
White rice
Wine vinegar
Worcestershire sauce

Spirits:
Brandy
Madeira
Port wine
Rum
Sherry, dry
Triple Sec
White wine, dry

APPETEASERS
(Appetizers)

Gratin of Crab

40 minutes

Step One:
1/2 cup milk
1/2 jalapeño, minced
1/2 tsp. thyme
1 bay leaf
1 tsp. minced parsley
salt and pepper to taste
1 cup fresh coarse bread crumbs

Preheat oven to 325° F. Combine milk, jalapeño, and herbs in a small saucepan over medium-high heat and bring to a boil. Season with salt and pepper. Reduce heat and simmer 10 minutes. Strain liquid into bowl, add bread crumbs to bowl, and set aside 10 minutes.

Step Two:
3 slices bacon, cut in half
1 1/2 Tbsp. sliced green onion
1/2 jalapeño, minced
1 1/2 Tbsp. snipped fresh chives
1 1/2 Tbsp. minced fresh parsley
1/2 tsp. thyme
1/2 tsp. basil
1/2 lb. fresh crabmeat

Fry bacon, onion, and jalapeño until bacon is crisp. Remove and drain on paper towels. In a large bowl, combine bacon mixture and herbs. Squeeze bread crumb mixture from Step One until dry and combine with bacon mixture. Drain crabmeat in colander or pat dry with paper towels. Fold crab into bacon and bread crumb mixture.

Step Three:
2 Tbsp. butter
4 tsp. fresh lime juice
1 Tbsp. rum
2 Tbsp. finely grated Gruyère cheese
1/2 avocado, sliced
lime wedges

In large frying pan over medium heat, sauté crab mixture in butter until browned. Blend in lime juice and rum. Butter two small scallop shells or individual baking dishes. Divide crab mixture between dishes and sprinkle with cheese. Place on baking sheet and bake 10 minutes. Garnish with avocado slices and lime wedges. Serve immediately.

Artichoke Balls

Step One:

1 six-oz. jar marinated
  artichoke hearts
4 canned artichoke hearts, drained
2 eggs
1 large clove garlic, minced
2 tsp. Worcestershire sauce
1/4 tsp. liquid smoke
1/4 tsp. Tabasco
1 cup Italian bread crumbs
3/4 cup Parmesan cheese

Lightly grease a baking sheet. Drain marinated artichoke hearts, reserving marinade. Combine with canned artichoke hearts, mince, and set aside. Beat eggs with 2 Tablespoons of the reserved marinade. Add garlic, Worcestershire sauce, liquid smoke, and Tabasco, and blend well. Add artichokes and bread crumbs to this mixture. Using your hands, roll the dough into 1" balls and roll them in Parmesan cheese. These taste best if they sit for several hours before baking. Cover and chill until ready to bake. Preheat oven to 325° F. Bake for 7–10 minutes.

Stuffed Grape Leaves

Step One:

6 dried apricots, finely chopped
2 Tbsp. coarsely chopped walnuts
1/4 lb. ground lamb
3 Tbsp. uncooked white rice
1 green onion, chopped
2 tsp. snipped fresh chives
1/8 tsp. cinnamon
1 eight-oz. jar grape leaves, rinsed
  and patted dry
fresh lemon juice

Combine all ingredients—except the grape leaves and lemon juice—in a bowl. Mix well. Lay grape leaf with veins up on a flat surface, stems facing you. Place 1 Tablespoon of filling at the base of the leaf and roll, tucking the sides in neatly. Place seam side down in a saucepan. Repeat until all the filling is used. Sprinkle with lemon juice, cover with water, and bring to a boil. Turn flame to low, simmer 1 hour.

Step Two:

mint jelly
currant jelly

Remove stuffed grape leaves from pan and cool slightly. Place unused grape leaves on salad plate, top with three or four stuffed grape leaves. Put a dollop of mint jelly on one side and a dollop of currant jelly on the other. Serve.

Crab and Shrimp Duet

2 hours, 40 minutes

Step One:

1/4 tsp. paprika
3 Tbsp. olive oil
1–2 anchovy fillets, mashed
1 tsp. Dijon mustard
1 tsp. fresh lemon juice
1/3 cup sliced celery
2 Tbsp. minced fresh parsley
1 Tbsp. snipped fresh chives

Whisk paprika, oil, anchovies, mustard, and lemon juice together until well blended. Add celery, parsley, and chives. Blend thoroughly.

Step Two:

1 cup medium shrimp, shelled, deveined, and cooked
1 cup cooked crabmeat
lettuce leaves (red leaf, butter, or iceberg) for garnish
1 Tbsp. chopped fresh parsley

Toss shrimp with dressing from Step One to coat. Gently fold in crab. Cover and marinate 2 hours in refrigerator. Let stand at room temperature for 30 minutes prior to serving. Place one or two lettuce leaves on chilled salad plates. Mound crab and shrimp mixture in center of plates and garnish with a sprinkle of parsley.

Bacon-Wrapped Scallops

1 hour, 30 minutes

Step One:

4 slices lean bacon

Bring a saucepan filled halfway with water to a boil. Add bacon and cook 2–3 minutes. Remove bacon and drain on paper towels.

Step Two:

3 Tbsp. bourbon
2 Tbsp. soy sauce
2 Tbsp. brown sugar
2 Tbsp. chopped green onion
1 Tbsp. hot horseradish
prepared mustard
dash of Worcestershire sauce
12 sea scallops, halved

Combine all ingredients—except the scallops—in a bowl. Add scallops and marinate one hour. Remove scallops from marinade. Thread bacon and scallops on skewers, starting with bacon and interlacing it over and under each scallop. Grill over high heat until bacon is crispy, about 10 minutes. Turn frequently.

Sautéed Camembert

Step One:

1 eight-oz. round of Camembert
cheese

Let cheese stand at room temperature for 15 minutes.

Step Two:

1/3 cup Japanese bread crumbs or
fine dry bread crumbs
1/2 tsp. Spice Islands fines herbes
1 egg, beaten

Mix bread crumbs and fines herbes together. Spread mixture out on a plate. Coat the cheese with egg, then roll the cheese in the crumb mixture.

Step Three:

3 Tbsp. butter
1 Tbsp. chopped fresh chives
French bread, sliced

Melt butter in small frying pan over low heat. Increase heat to medium and sauté cheese in butter 1–2 minutes, until brown. Turn and brown 1 minute on other side. (If cheese begins to melt, turn it immediately). Place on serving tray and sprinkle with chives. Surround with small slices of French bread.

Spinacheez

1 hour

Step One:

1 Tbsp. butter
1/4 cup minced leek
1 ten-oz. pkg. frozen chopped
   spinach, thawed and squeezed dry
1/3 cup feta cheese
1/3 cup minced fresh parsley
1/4 tsp. dill
1 egg, beaten
salt and pepper to taste

Melt butter in frying pan over medium heat. Sauté leek until tender. Mix in spinach and sauté until heated through. Turn the mixture into a bowl, add feta, parsley, and dill and mix well. Blend in egg and season with salt and pepper.

Step Two:

1/2 cup butter, melted
1 pkg. phyllo leaves

Preheat oven to 425° F. Lightly butter a baking sheet. Place one sheet of phyllo dough on a work surface. Cut dough into 2" wide strips and brush the strips with melted butter. Cover all but one of the strips with wax paper and a damp towel. Place a teaspoon of the filling on the end of the phyllo dough strip and fold, forming a small triangle. Continue folding until you get to the end of the strip. Brush the triangle with butter and place it on the baking sheet. Repeat process until you have used all the filling. Work quickly. When finished, brush the triangles with melted butter and bake for 15 minutes.

Step Three:

fresh dill sprigs
cherry tomatoes

Arrange the triangles on a serving tray. Garnish with dill and cherry tomatoes. Serve hot.

LESS THAN SUBTLE SEDUCTIONS
(Salad and Soup)

Your salad should be an extension of your uninhibited spirit. We encourage you to show a bit of daring. Our avocado-based dressing is boldly different in appearance, yet mild enough to complement the most delicately flavored entrée. For a triumphant departure from the expected, serve our spinach salad with roasted peppers and Portobello mushrooms. If you're looking for a delicate, refreshing alternative, splash our creamy lemon vinaigrette on snow peas, pears, and avocados. An innovative composition of greens served with a mouth-watering dressing will reflect your confidence in the evening to come. Or, if you're not in the mood for greens, try the deliciously different Sweet Potato Soup for a warm and satiny temptation that will thaw any of your companion's inhibitions.

Hanky Panky Greens
45 minutes

Crisp Garden Salad with Silky Avocado Dressing

Step One:

2 eggs
1/4 lb. fresh green beans
1/2 head butter lettuce, washed
  and dried
1/2 head red leaf lettuce, washed
  and dried
1 cup thinly sliced mushrooms
4 artichoke hearts, quartered
6 radishes, minced
1/2 cup crispy chow mein noodles

Hard-boil the eggs. Break off the ends of the green beans. Cut the beans diagonally into 1" pieces. Steam the beans until they are crisp-tender, about 18 minutes. Plunge the beans into ice water to stop the cooking and set their color. Tear lettuces into bite-size pieces. Toss in remaining ingredients.

Step Two:

1/2 avocado
1/4 cup sour cream
3 Tbsp. whipping cream
1/2 tsp. minced garlic
1 Tbsp. plain yogurt
1 Tbsp. red wine vinegar
1/4 tsp. salt
Tabasco
milk, as needed

Combine avocado, sour cream, whipping cream, garlic, yogurt, and vinegar in blender and blend until smooth. Season with salt and Tabasco to taste. Thin with a little milk if necessary. Toss with greens and serve.

Are You Game? Greens

40 minutes

Spinach, Roasted Pepper, and Portobello Mushroom Salad
with Fines Herbes Vinaigrette

Step One:

1/4 cup rice wine vinegar
3/4 cup light olive oil
1 1/2 Tbsp. chopped fresh thyme
1 Tbsp. minced fresh parsley
1 tsp. chopped fresh chives
1/2 tsp. salt
1/2 tsp. white pepper
1/2 tsp. marjoram
1/2 tsp. tarragon

Combine ingredients in a small bowl and whisk until blended.

Step Two:

1 red bell pepper, halved and seeded
1 yellow bell pepper, halved
   and seeded

Grill peppers or roast them over an open flame using tongs, until the skin chars and blisters. Put peppers in a paper bag and seal tightly. Allow them to steam for 15 minutes. Remove from bag and chop coarsely.

Step Three:

1 Portobello mushroom, diced
1 Tbsp. butter
1/2 lb. fresh spinach, washed and
   squeezed dry
2 Tbsp. chopped sundried tomatoes
Parmesan cheese

Sauté mushroom in butter over high heat until tender. Tear spinach into bite-size pieces. Gently toss spinach, mushroom, peppers, and tomatoes with dressing, and divide salad between two salad plates. Generously grate Parmesan over salads and serve.

Say Yes Salad

40 minutes

Pear and Snow Pea Salad with Lemon Vinaigrette

Step One:

1 egg

2 Tbsp. rice wine vinegar

1 Tbsp. finely chopped celery leaves

2 tsp. sugar

1/2 tsp. oregano

salt and pepper to taste

1/3 cup plus 1 Tbsp. light olive oil

2 Tbsp. fresh lemon juice

Combine ingredients—except the olive oil—in a bowl and whisk thoroughly. Add oil in a thin steady stream, whisking constantly until completely blended.

Step Two:

2–4 oz. snow peas, trimmed and strings removed

1/2 head romaine lettuce

1/2 head butter lettuce

1 small head Belgian endive

1 Comice pear, peeled and diced

1 avocado, pitted and diced

2 Tbsp. roasted salted sunflower seeds

2 Tbsp. freshly grated Parmesan cheese

Slice snow peas diagonally into bite-size pieces. Drop them into boiling water and cook until crisp-tender, about 3 minutes. Drain snow peas and plunge them into ice water to stop the cooking and set their color. Wash and dry lettuces. Tear butter and romaine into bite-size pieces. Separate endive leaves. Gently toss romaine and butter lettuces, pear, snow peas, and avocado with dressing. Fan endive leaves on salad plates. Mound salad at base of endive. Sprinkle with sunflower seeds and Parmesan. Serve.

20

Sweet Potato Soup

Step One:

3 small sweet potatoes

Preheat oven to 400° F. Prick sweet potatoes with fork, place in baking dish, and bake 1 hour.

Step Two:

2 cups low-salt chicken broth
1/2 cup sliced leeks
1/4 cup whipping cream
1 tsp. marsala wine
1 Tbsp. minced fresh parsley
1 tsp. basil
pinch cayenne
parsley sprigs
2 Tbsp. sour cream

Combine chicken broth and leeks in saucepan over medium heat. Simmer until leeks are tender. Pour into food processor. Scoop sweet potato from skins and add to processor. Purée until smooth. Return to pan, bring to a boil, and reduce heat. Add cream, wine, minced parsley, basil, and cayenne, and simmer 5 minutes. Ladle into small bowls, garnish with parsley sprigs and dollop of sour cream.

PIÈCE DE NO RESISTANCE
(Entrées)

♥Play Hard To Get

45 minutes

. . . but make sure you're easy to catch!

Sassy Spinach and Shrimp Salad with Exotic Curry Dressing

Step One:

1/3 cup light olive oil
2 Tbsp. wine vinegar
1/2 tsp. sugar
1/4–1/2 tsp. curry powder
1/4 tsp. garlic salt
1 Tbsp. dry white wine
1 tsp. soy sauce
1/2 tsp. dry mustard
1/4 tsp. salt
1/2 tsp. freshly ground pepper

Combine ingredients in a jar, cover, and shake until well blended.

Step Two:

10 peppercorns
1 lemon, sliced
4 celery ribs, chopped
2 bay leaves
1 lb. medium shrimp, shelled and
    deveined

Pour 3 quarts of water into a stockpot. Add Step Two ingredients—except shrimp—and bring to a boil. Add shrimp. Turn heat to simmer and cook until shrimp are just pink. Remove shrimp from pot with a slotted spoon and allow to cool. Discard remaining contents of pot.

Step Three:

1 lb. fresh young spinach, torn
1 lb. bacon, fried crisp and coarsely
    chopped
1 red onion, thinly sliced
6 hard-boiled eggs, chopped
1/4 lb. mushrooms, sliced

Toss Step Three ingredients with dressing from Step One. Divide salad ingredients between two chilled plates. Fan shrimp on top of spinach in a circle. Serve.

Appeteaser

Bacon-Wrapped Scallops

Less Than Subtle Seduction

Sweet Potato Soup

Pièce de No Resistance

Play Hard To Get

Something on the Side

Lemon Rice

Wine

Chenin Blanc

♥Shanghai Alibi

This may give you the time you need to realize your lover's fantasies.

Grilled Chicken, Pear, and Toasted Almond Salad with Ginger-Lime Dressing

Step One:
1/4 cup red wine vinegar
1 Tbsp. fresh lime juice
1 tsp. grated fresh ginger
1/4 tsp. chili oil
1 Tbsp. corn oil
1/2 cup light olive oil
freshly ground pepper to taste
salt to taste

Preheat grill to medium-high heat. Combine vinegar, lime juice, and ginger in a mixing bowl. Whisk in oils until well blended. Season with salt and pepper.

Step Two:
1 lb. chicken breasts, skinned
 and boned

Flatten chicken breasts with a mallet. Brush breasts with some of the dressing from Step One. Grill chicken until the juices run clear when the chicken is pierced with a fork and the meat is lightly springy when touched. Slice chicken into thin strips.

Step Three:
1 head romaine lettuce, washed
1/2 lb. mixed greens (watercress,
 radicchio, arugula, endive,
 or spinach)
1 pear, peeled and diced
1 avocado, diced
3/4 cup sliced water chestnuts
1/3 cup toasted slivered almonds

Slice romaine into 1/2" strips. Toss romaine and mixed greens with enough dressing from Step One to coat. Add pears, avocados, and water chestnuts, and toss gently. Divide mixture onto two chilled plates. Arrange chicken on top of greens. Drizzle with a little more dressing and sprinkle with almonds.

Appeteaser

Sautéed Camembert

Less Than Subtle Seduction

Sweet Potato Soup

Pièce de No Resistance

♥*Shanghai Alibi*

Something on the Side

Lemon Rice

Wine

Gewürztraminer

Fantasies Au Fruits de Mer

Ancient mariners have long held fantasies of the deep. To what depths do your fantasies go?

Fettuccine Tossed with Scallops, Shrimp, Ham, and Vegetables

Step One:

1/2 cup olive oil
1 clove garlic, minced
1/4 cup fresh lemon juice
8–10 drops Tabasco
1/4 cup chopped fresh dill
2 Tbsp. chopped leek
3 Tbsp. chopped fresh parsley
1 tsp. freshly ground pepper
2 firm small tomatoes, chopped
1/2 cup julienne ham
1/2 cup frozen baby peas

Combine all ingredients—except ham and peas—in a large bowl. Mix thoroughly. Fold in ham and peas.

Step Two:

1/2 lb. fresh shrimp, peeled and deveined
1/2 lb. fresh ocean scallops

Boil water in stockpot. Drop shrimp in and cook for 1 minute, or until pink. Remove shrimp immediately from stockpot, using a slotted spoon, and add to dressing from Step One. Add scallops to stockpot. Cook, stirring, until almost opaque. Remove scallops from pot, drain, and add to shrimp and dressing.

Step Three:

8–10 oz. fettuccine
1/4 cup chopped pistachio nuts

Cook pasta according to package directions until al dente. Add fettuccine to seafood and dressing, toss gently, and spoon into warmed au gratin dishes. Top with pistachio nuts and serve immediately.

SUGGESTED MENU

Appeteaser

Gratin of Crab

Less Than Subtle Seduction

Hanky Panky Greens

Pièce de No Resistance

Fantasies Au Fruits de Mer

Something on the Side

Artichoke Fromage

Wine

Sauvignon Blanc

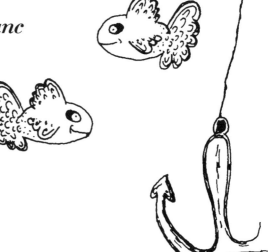

Peel Me a Grape

We couldn't remember if this was what Cleopatra said to Marc Antony or if Mae West coined the phrase. But we are sure that whoever said it knew what they were suggesting.

Linguine and Scallops in Tarragon Cream Sauce

Step One:

2 Tbsp. butter
2 Tbsp. light olive oil
3/4 lb. fresh ocean scallops, quartered
1 cup seedless green grapes

Heat butter and olive oil over medium heat. Add scallops and grapes and sauté until scallops become opaque, about 2 minutes. Transfer scallops and grapes to a bowl.

Step Two:

8-10 oz. linguine
2 large leeks, chopped
2 cloves garlic, minced
10 mushrooms, sliced
1 tsp. basil
3/4 tsp. tarragon
1/2 tsp. thyme
1/2 tsp. chervil
2 Tbsp. flour
3/4 cup dry white wine
1/2 cup whipping cream
1/2 tsp. sugar
salt and pepper to taste

Cook linguine according to package directions until al dente. Meanwhile, add leeks to pan and sauté until limp. Add garlic, mushrooms, and herbs, and continue cooking for 5 minutes. Whisk flour into sauce. Add wine and whisk sauce until thickened. Add cream and sugar and season with salt and pepper. Return scallops and grapes to pan, stirring gently to coat with sauce.

Step Three:

1/2 avocado, cut into bite-size pieces

Put linguine in warmed au gratin dishes. Spoon sauce over pasta, and sprinkle with avocado pieces.

SUGGESTED MENU

Appeteaser

Artichoke Balls

Less Than Subtle Seduction

Say Yes Salad

Pièce de No Resistance

Peel Me a Grape

Something on the Side

Pistachio Carrots

Wine

Fumé Blanc

Fools Rush In

. . . or so they say. Let's feast all night and play all day.

Pasta with Mixed Grilled Peppers in Creamy Lemon-Dill Sauce

Step One:

2 carrots, peeled and sliced
1 leek, cut into 1" pieces
1/2 onion, quartered
4 ribs celery, cut into 1" pieces
3 bay leaves
3/4 Tbsp. peppercorns
1 tsp. thyme
1 can diced tomatoes (do not drain)
1/2 head romaine lettuce, chopped

Combine ingredients with 3 quarts water in stockpot. Bring to a boil, reduce heat, and simmer for 1 1/2 hours. Pour stock into a bowl through a strainer, pressing on vegetables to get all juices out.

Step Two:

1 red bell pepper, halved and seeded
1 green bell pepper, halved and seeded
1 yellow bell pepper, halved and seeded

Grill or roast peppers under the broiler or over an open flame using tongs until the skin chars and blisters. Put peppers in a paper bag and seal tightly. Allow to steam for 15 minutes. Remove and slice peppers diagonally into 1/2" strips. Then slice the strips diagonally in the opposite direction to form 1/2" diamond-shaped pieces.

Step Three:

1 large tomato, chopped
1 Tbsp. chopped green onion
1–2 cloves garlic, minced
2 Tbsp. butter
1/2–1 tsp. fresh lemon juice
1 Tbsp. dill

Sauté peppers, tomato, onion, and garlic in butter until garlic is lightly browned. Add 2 1/2 cups of stock from Step One. Boil mixture, stirring frequently, until reduced by half. Add lemon juice and dill to reduced sauce.

Step Four:

1 lb. pasta such as fusilli (long
   springs) or farfalle (bow ties)
6 Tbsp. butter

Cook pasta according to package directions until al dente. Drain. Slowly whisk butter into sauce from Step Three until creamy. Spoon sauce over hot pasta and serve.

Appeteaser

Stuffed Grape Leaves

Less Than Subtle Seduction

Say Yes Salad

Pièce de No Resistance

Fools Rush In

Something on the Side

Vegetable Sauté

Wine

Sauvignon Blanc

Love Knots

I'm all tied up in knots over you.

Smoky Prosciutto, Walnut, and Roquefort Pasta

Step One:

6 thin slices prosciutto, minced
1 1/2 cups large walnut pieces
4 oz. Roquefort or bleu cheese, crumbled
2/3 cup minced fresh parsley
2 Tbsp. minced fresh rosemary
2 cloves garlic, finely minced
1 tsp. freshly ground pepper
1/2 cup light olive oil

Combine ingredients in a large bowl, blending well. Set aside. This tastes best when the flavors are allowed to blend for 1 or 2 hours.

Step Two:

1 lb. pasta (linguine, fettuccine, spaghetti, or tagliatelle)
3–4 rosemary sprigs

Cook pasta according to package directions until al dente. Drain and immediately toss with sauce. Serve on warm plates garnished with sprigs of fresh rosemary.

SUGGESTED MENU

Appeteaser

Stuffed Grape Leaves

Less Than Subtle Seduction

Are You Game? Greens

Pièce de No Resistance

♥*Love Knots*

Something on the Side

Artichoke Fromage

Wine

Sauvignon Blanc

Bedroom Brochette

50 minutes

It's a short distance from the dining room to the bedroom. Get there faster with this entreé!

Marinated Shrimp and Scallop Brochette

Step One:

8–10 slices bacon

Cook bacon over medium-low heat until half done and still limp.

Step Two:

1/2 lb. mushrooms, cleaned
1/2 lb. large shrimp, cleaned and deveined
1/2 lb. ocean scallops

While bacon is still warm, begin threading skewers. Thread mushrooms, shrimp, and scallops onto skewers, interlacing bacon between each. Anchor each end of the skewer with a mushroom.

Step Three:

1/3 cup olive oil
2 Tbsp. fresh lemon juice
1/2 cup butter, melted
1 Tbsp. dill
1/2 tsp. salt
1/4 tsp. freshly ground pepper

Combine ingredients in small mixing bowl. Place skewers on baking sheet and generously brush them with marinade. (At this point, you may refrigerate the skewers for up to three hours.)

Step Four:

lemon wedges

If you are going to barbecue the brochettes, clean and oil the grill, and light the coals. If you are going to broil them, preheat the broiler. Grill brochettes four to six inches from heat. Baste them frequently, turning them as needed to prevent burning, until scallops are opaque and bacon is done, about 5 minutes. Serve with lemon wedges.

34

SUGGESTED MENU

Appeteaser

Sautéed Camembert

Less Than Subtle Seduction

Sweet Potato Soup

Pièce de No Resistance

Bedroom Brochette

Something on the Side

Lemon Rice and Pistachio Carrots

Wine

Fumé Blanc

♥ One Night Stand

A one night stand may be all she wants, but this one could earn you an encore!

Baked Shrimp in Wine-Garlic Sauce

Step One:

6 Tbsp. butter, melted
1/4 cup white wine
2 Tbsp. minced fresh parsley
2 Tbsp. fresh lemon juice
3 large cloves garlic, minced
2 tsp. basil
1 tsp. Worcestershire
1/2 tsp. Tabasco

Preheat oven to 425° F. Combine ingredients in a mixing bowl. Set aside 1/4 cup of mixture.

Step Two:

1 lb. medium shrimp, peeled and
  deveined
1/2 cup dried, fine bread crumbs
lemon slices
parsley sprigs

Divide shrimp into au gratin dishes. Spoon sauce from Step One over shrimp. Combine reserved 1/4 cup sauce with bread crumbs and toss gently. Sprinkle mixture over shrimp. Bake 10 minutes or until shrimp turn bright pink. Top with lemon slices and garnish with parsley sprigs.

Appeteaser

Sautéed Camembert

Less Than Subtle Seduction

Say Yes Salad

Pièce de No Resistance

♥One Night Stand

Something on the Side

Lemon Rice and
Vegetable Sauté

Wine

Gewürztraminer

Sea Nymph Promise

25 minutes

*Greek legend has it that a sea nymph, Calypso, promised her lovers immortality
if they would never leave her. You, of course, should negotiate your own terms!*

Shrimp in Feta-Tomato Sauce

Step One:

3 Tbsp. butter
1 leek, chopped
2 Tbsp. minced fresh parsley
6 mushrooms, sliced
1 large tomato, chopped
1/2 tsp. oregano
salt and pepper to taste
2 Tbsp. sherry

Melt butter in saucepan over medium heat. Add leek, parsley, and mushrooms, stirring until they are soft. Add tomato and oregano, season with salt and pepper. Simmer until reduced by half. Blend in sherry, turn heat to high, and boil 2 minutes.

Step Two:

3 Tbsp. butter
2 cloves garlic, minced
3/4 lb. medium shrimp, peeled and
  deveined
4 oz. feta cheese, crumbled
2 Tbsp. chopped fresh parsley

Melt butter in large frying pan over medium heat. Add garlic and stir for 30 seconds to release its aroma. Add shrimp and stir until pink. Bring tomato mixture to a boil, add shrimp mixture and 3 ounces feta cheese. Heat through. Spoon into warmed au gratin dishes. Garnish with remaining feta and parsley.

Appeteaser

Artichoke Balls

Less Than Subtle Seduction

Say Yes Salad

Pièce de No Resistance

♥*Sea Nymph Promise*

Something on the Side

Lemon Rice and Vegetable Sauté

Wine

Fumé Blanc

♥ *Thyming Is Everything*

... and tonight's the night!

Spicy Pecan and Herb Orange Roughy

Step One:

1 bay leaf, crumbled
1 Tbsp. cayenne
1 Tbsp. paprika
3/4 tsp. onion powder
3/4 tsp. basil
1/2 tsp. black pepper
1/2 tsp. white pepper
1/2 tsp. garlic powder
1/4 tsp. thyme
1/4 tsp. tarragon
1/4 tsp. hot dry mustard
1/8 tsp. oregano
1/8 tsp. crushed rosemary

Combine herbs and spices in an airtight jar and set aside.

Step Two:

1 Tbsp. butter
1/2 cup coarsely chopped pecans
1/4 tsp. thyme
1/4 tsp. oregano
1/4 tsp. herbs and spices mix
   (from Step One)
1/8 tsp. allspice

Melt butter in small frying pan over medium heat. Mix remaining ingredients together in a small bowl and add to pan. Sauté mixture until pecans are golden brown. Cover, keep warm.

Step Three:

1/4 cup dry white wine
2 Tbsp. white wine vinegar
2 Tbsp. finely chopped onion
2 Tbsp. heavy cream
1 large tomato, skinned and chopped
2 Tbsp. butter, melted
1 lb. orange roughy fillets or other
   firm white fish
1/4 tsp. herbs and spices mix (from
   Step One)

In small saucepan over high heat, bring wine, vinegar, and onion to a boil. Cook until almost all liquid is gone. Add cream and three-fourths of the tomatoes. Turn heat to low and simmer while cooking the fish. Start grill or barbecue. Brush butter over fillets. Sprinkle fish with herbs and spices mix. Grill 2–3 minutes per side. Ladle sauce onto warmed plates. Lay fillets on top of sauce, sprinkle pecans over them, and sprinkle remaining tomatoes over pecans. Serve.

Appeteaser

Shrimp Balls

Less Than Subtle Seductions

Hanky Panky Greens

and Sweet Potato Soup

Pièce de No Resistance

♥ *Thyming Is Everything*

Something on the Side

Pistachio Carrots

Wine

Sauvignon Blanc

A Coy Catch

Don't let the best one get away!

Snapper in Fresh Herb Cream Sauce

Step One:

4 Tbsp. butter
1/4 cup flour
1/2 tsp. salt
1/2 tsp. pepper
2 snapper fillets, patted dry

Preheat oven to 400° F. Butter flameproof baking dish. In large frying pan over medium heat, melt butter. Combine flour with salt and pepper in a plastic bag. Add snapper to bag and shake to coat. Add snapper to pan and brown on both sides. Remove snapper to baking dish.

Step Two:

1/4 cup minced onion
3/4 cup white wine
3/4 tsp. chervil
1/2 tsp. tarragon
1 tsp. basil
1 Tbsp. minced fresh parsley
1 Tbsp. snipped fresh chives
3/4 cup whipping cream
salt and pepper to taste
paprika

Turn heat to low. Add onion to frying pan and sauté until limp. Add wine to pan, turn heat to high, and boil. Add chervil, tarragon, basil, parsley, chives, and whipping cream. Season with salt and pepper. Pour over snapper and bake until snapper is opaque, about 8 minutes, basting occasionally. Transfer snapper to heated plates. Place baking dish over high heat, bring to a boil, and reduce liquid by half. Pour sauce over snapper, dust with paprika, and serve.

SUGGESTED MENU

Appeteaser

Crab and Shrimp Duet

Less Than Subtle Seduction

Say Yes Salad

Pièce de No Resistance

A Coy Catch

Something on the Side

Carrot-Potato Au Gratin

Wine

Chardonnay

Flirtatious Fillets

Flirting can pay and go a long way. Just be prepared to roll in the hay!

Salmon Fillets in Radish-Dill Sauce

Step One:

1/2 cup dry white wine
1/2 cup whipping cream
2 Tbsp. minced leek
1 cup butter
6 radishes, minced
2 Tbsp. chopped fresh dill
1 Tbsp. prepared horseradish
salt to taste
1/4 tsp. white pepper

To saucepan over medium heat, add wine, cream, and leek. Bring to a boil, stirring until reduced by half. Turn heat to low, and whisk in butter 2 Tablespoons at a time. Stir in radishes, dill, horseradish, salt, and pepper. Turn off heat.

Step Two:

1/2 cup milk
1/3 cup flour
1 Tbsp. butter
1 Tbsp. olive oil
2 salmon fillets
2 radishes, thinly sliced
2 dill sprigs

Pour milk into pie pan. Put flour in another pan. Melt butter and oil in frying pan over medium heat. Dip salmon in milk, then in flour. Add salmon to pan and sauté until golden brown. Turn salmon and sauté other side until fish is almost opaque. Ladle a little sauce into warmed au gratin dishes. Top with salmon. Nap salmon with sauce and garnish with radish slices and dill. Serve immediately.

SUGGESTED MENU

Appeteaser

Spinacheez

Less Than Subtle Seduction

Say Yes Salad

Pièce de No Resistance

Flirtatious Fillets

Something on the Side

Artichoke Fromage

Wine

Chardonnay

♥ Chicken Aphrodisia

1 hour

Give the rooster a booster and the chicken a delight!

Sautéed Strips of Chicken and Vegetables in Béarnaise Sauce

Step One:

1/2 cup butter
1 cup chopped onion
1 leek, chopped
2 cloves garlic, minced
2 red potatoes, peeled and cut in
   1/2" cubes
1 cup cubed ham
1 cup sliced mushrooms
1/2 cup white wine
1 Tbsp. minced fresh parsley

Preheat oven to 200° F. Melt butter in large frying pan over medium heat. Add onion, leek, garlic, and potatoes. Sauté for 15 minutes or until golden brown. Add ham, mushrooms, wine, and parsley. Continue cooking until mushrooms give up their juices. Spoon mixture into ovenproof serving dish. Cover and keep warm in oven.

Step Two:

3/4 cup flour
1 tsp. salt
1/2 tsp. freshly ground pepper
1/4 tsp. cayenne
1 chicken breast
2 chicken legs
3 Tbsp. corn oil

Combine flour, salt, pepper, and cayenne in plastic bag. Bone, skin, and cut chicken breast and legs into 1" x 1 1/2" strips. Add chicken strips to plastic bag in batches; shake to coat. Add corn oil to pan and sauté chicken over medium heat until golden brown. Drain on paper towels. Arrange on top of vegetable mixture, cover, and return to oven.

Step Three:

1 1/2 Tbsp. minced leek
1/4 tsp. minced garlic
2 tsp. fresh lemon juice
1/3 cup white wine
1 1/2 tsp. chervil
1 1/2 tsp. tarragon
1/4 tsp. white pepper

Combine ingredients and cook over medium heat until reduced to 3 Tablespoons.

Step Four:

1/3 cup white wine
3 egg yolks
1/8 tsp. cayenne
1/2 cup butter, melted

Put wine, egg yolks, and cayenne in blender and mix for 2 seconds. Add reduced herb mixture, turn blender on high speed, and add butter in a slow stream. Continue blending until the mixture is thickened slightly. Pour over chicken and serve.

SUGGESTED MENU

Appeteaser

Artichoke Balls

Less Than Subtle Seductions

Say Yes Salad

and Sweet Potato Soup

Pièce de No Resistance

♥*Chicken Aphrodisia*

Something on the Side

Pistachio Carrots

Wine

Chardonnay

A Little Dill Will Do

It isn't how much you use, it's how you use it!

Chicken in Lemon-Dill Sauce

Step One:

2 Tbsp. butter
1 Tbsp. fresh lemon juice
1 clove garlic, minced
1/8 tsp. white pepper
1/4 tsp. paprika
2 Tbsp. chopped fresh dill
10–12 button mushrooms, stems
  removed
3 Tbsp. dry white wine
2 chicken breasts, boned and skinned

Melt butter in frying pan over medium heat. Add the lemon juice, garlic, pepper, paprika, dill, mushrooms, and wine. Bring just to boiling point and turn heat to low. Add chicken, turning to coat. Cover and simmer 20 minutes.

Step Two:

1 Tbsp. flour
1/2 cup whipping cream
dill sprigs

Remove chicken to warm au gratin dishes. Whisk flour into wine sauce. Cook, whisking constantly, for 2 minutes. Blend in cream and warm through. Nap chicken with sauce and garnish with fresh dill sprigs. Serve immediately.

SUGGESTED MENU

Appeteaser

Crab and Shrimp Duet

Less Than Subtle Seduction

Hanky Panky Greens

Pièce de No Resistance

A Little Dill Will Do

Something on the Side

Carrot-Potato Au Gratin

Wine

Chenin Blanc

♥Exotic Erotic Chicken

1 hour, 30 minutes

Set the trap with exotic bait and erotic game may be your catch!

Herb-Crusted Chicken in Paprika and Sherry Cream Sauce

Step One:

2 Tbsp. butter
1/2 cup flour
1 tsp. paprika
1/8 tsp. cayenne
1/8 tsp. ginger
1/4 tsp. basil
1/4 tsp. chervil
1/8 tsp. nutmeg
1 tsp. salt
1/4 tsp. freshly ground pepper
4–6 chicken thighs or 2 chicken
    breasts, skinned

Preheat oven to 325° F. In a large frying pan over medium heat, melt butter. Put flour, spices, herbs, and seasonings in plastic bag and shake. Add chicken, one piece at a time, and shake to coat. Add chicken to frying pan and brown on all sides. Drain chicken on paper towels, then put in a baking dish.

Step Two:

1 large clove garlic, minced
5 mushrooms, sliced
3/4 cup chicken stock
1 Tbsp. Worcestershire sauce
1/4 cup dry sherry
4 artichoke hearts, quartered
1 cup sour cream
1/4 cup slivered almonds
2 Tbsp. minced fresh parsley

Add garlic and mushrooms to pan and sauté 2 minutes. Pour off excess butter. Add stock, Worcestershire, sherry, and artichokes. Heat through and pour over chicken. Bake, uncovered, for 1 hour. Remove chicken to warmed au gratin dishes, reserving sauce. Stir sour cream into sauce and ladle over chicken. Garnish with almonds and parsley.

SUGGESTED MENU

Appeteaser

Gratin of Crab

Less Than Subtle Seduction

Say Yes Salad

Pièce de No Resistance

♥*Exotic Erotic Chicken*

Something on the Side

Carrot-Potato Au Gratin

Wine

Chardonnay

♥Birds in Bondage

Decidedly kinky! Reserve this one for only your most uninhibited evenings.

Chicken Thighs Stuffed with Raisins, Walnuts, and Wild Rice

Step One:

1 cup uncooked wild rice
4–6 boned chicken thighs
1/4 cup raisins
1/2 cup chopped walnuts

Cook rice according to package directions. Flatten chicken with a mallet or rolling pin. Spoon approximately 1/4 cup rice onto each piece of chicken. Cover remaining rice to keep warm, and set aside. Place equal amounts of raisins and nuts on each piece of chicken, then roll each piece like a jelly roll. Secure with thread or toothpicks.

Step Two:

2 Tbsp. butter
1/4 cup water

Heat butter in large frying pan, add chicken rolls, and brown them over medium heat. Add water, cover, and simmer 15 minutes.

Step Three:

1/4 cup packed brown sugar
2 Tbsp. cornstarch
1/4 tsp. cinnamon
1 3/4 cups water
1 tsp. fresh lemon juice
1 tsp. salt
1/2 cup raisins

Remove chicken rolls to a plate. Mix brown sugar, cornstarch, and cinnamon together, and stir into liquid in pan. Add remaining ingredients and bring to a boil, stirring until thickened. Remove thread or toothpicks from chicken and return to pan. Cover and heat thoroughly.

Step Four:

2 Tbsp. fresh parsley

Using the reserved rice, create a bed of rice in two au gratin dishes. Divide chicken rolls between dishes, spoon sauce over chicken, and garnish with parsley.

SUGGESTED MENU

Appeteaser

Spinacheez

Less Than Subtle Seduction

Hanky Panky Greens

Pièce de No Resistance

Birds in Bondage

Something on the Side

Apple Yams

Wine

Gewürztraminer

Suite Talk

Come up and see me some time!

Chicken Breasts in Madeira-Chutney Sauce

Step One:

2 Tbsp. butter
2 chicken breasts, boned and
  skinned
1 leek, sliced
2 tsp. minced fresh ginger
3 Tbsp. fig, currant, and walnut
  chutney
1/3 cup Madeira
3/4 cup chicken broth

Melt butter in frying pan over medium heat. Add breasts and sauté about 5 minutes per side, or until springy to touch. Remove chicken to warmed platter; cover. Add leek, ginger, chutney, Madeira, and broth to pan. Turn heat to high and bring liquid to a boil. Stir constantly until reduced by half.

Step Two:

1/2 cup whipping cream
salt and pepper to taste
4 red leaf lettuce leaves
1 Tbsp. chopped fresh parsley
3 Tbsp. cashews

Pour chicken juices from platter into pan; add whipping cream. Boil over medium heat until slightly thickened. Season with salt and pepper. Lay lettuce leaves on plates, top with chicken breasts, spoon sauce over chicken, and sprinkle with parsley and cashews. Serve.

SUGGESTED MENU

Appeteaser

Spinacheez

Less Than Subtle Seduction

Say Yes Salad

Pièce de No Resistance

♥*Suite Talk*

Something on the Side

Apple Yams

Wine

Riesling

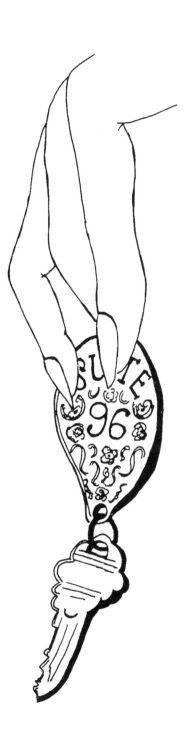

Racy Rendezvous

2 hours, 45 minutes

Get off to a fast start and finish in the first heat!

Rolled Veal Cutlets with Prosciutto and Herb Butter

Step One:

3 Tbsp. butter, at room temperature
1 Tbsp. minced fresh parsley
1 Tbsp. snipped fresh chives
1/2 tsp. marjoram
1 clove garlic, minced
1 Tbsp. grated fresh lemon zest
2–3 veal cutlets
2–3 slices prosciutto
2–3 slices Monterey Jack cheese

Blend butter, parsley, chives, marjoram, garlic, and lemon zest together. Spread on veal cutlets. Top each cutlet with a slice of prosciutto and a slice of cheese. Roll, starting from small end, and secure with toothpicks or string. Refrigerate 2–3 hours.

Step Two:

1 Tbsp. butter
1 Tbsp. oil
1/2 cup white wine

In a small saucepan over medium heat, melt butter and oil. Add veal to pan and brown veal on all sides. Add wine, cover, and simmer 10–15 minutes.

Step Three:

1 clove garlic, minced
1 Tbsp. butter
8 oz. fresh spinach, chopped, or
  1 ten-oz. pkg. frozen chopped
  spinach, thawed and drained

Sauté garlic in butter over medium heat for 2 minutes. Add spinach and sauté 1–2 minutes. Place spinach in warm au gratin dishes and top with veal rolls.

Step Four:

1 Tbsp. butter
2 Tbsp. pine nuts

Turn heat under wine sauce to high and boil until reduced by half. Add butter and whisk until slightly thickened. Spoon sauce over veal. Sprinkle with pine nuts.

SUGGESTED MENU

Appeteaser

Crab and Shrimp Duet

Less Than Subtle Seduction

Are You Game? Greens

Pièce de No Resistance

Racy Rendezvous

Something on the Side

Carrot-Potato Au Gratin

Wine

Gamay Beaujolais

Voyeur's Veal

. . . will excite the palate and the eye, but be careful; your epicurean friend may want to leave the lights on after dinner!

Sauté of Veal, Mushrooms, and Artichokes

Step One:

2 Tbsp. butter
1 cup artichoke hearts, quartered
6 mushrooms, thinly sliced
1 Tbsp. sliced green onions
1 Tbsp. fresh lemon juice
1 Tbsp. chopped fresh parsley

In large frying pan over medium heat, melt butter and sauté artichokes, mushrooms, and onions until onions and mushrooms soften. Add lemon juice and parsley, and turn heat to low while preparing veal.

Step Two:

1 Tbsp. butter
1 Tbsp. olive oil
1 tsp. salt
1 tsp. white pepper
2 Tbsp. flour
2 quarter-lb. veal cutlets
1 egg
1 Tbsp. water

In large frying pan over medium heat, melt butter and olive oil. Combine salt, pepper, and flour in plastic bag. Add veal and shake to coat. Beat egg and water together in pie pan. Dip both sides of veal in egg. Sauté veal 2 minutes per side and transfer to warmed au gratin dishes. Top with artichoke mixture. Serve.

SUGGESTED MENU

Appeteaser

Spinacheez

Less Than Subtle Seduction

Say Yes Salad

Pièce de No Resistance

Voyeur's Veal

Something on the Side

Pistachio Carrots

and Lemon Rice

Wine

Pinot Noir

Wok on the Wild Side

45 minutes

Live dangerously tonight!

Stir-Fry of Beef, Snow Peas, and Water Chestnuts

Step One:

1/4 tsp. sugar
2 tsp. soy sauce
1 tsp. freshly ground pepper
2 tsp. dry sherry
2 skirt steaks, unrolled and cut
   across grain into 1" x 1 1/2" slices
1 tsp. arrowroot
2 Tbsp. water
2 tsp. peanut oil

In a large glass baking pan, stir sugar, soy sauce, pepper, and sherry together. Add beef. Sprinkle mixture with arrowroot. Add 1 Tablespoon water and stir until it is too hard to stir. Add remaining 1 Tablespoon water and repeat process. Marinate beef in refrigerator for 30 minutes. Remove beef from pan and blend oil into reserved marinade.

Step Two:

1 tsp. arrowroot
6 Tbsp. beef stock
2 Tbsp. oyster sauce

In small bowl, thoroughly blend arrowroot, beef stock, and oyster sauce. Set aside.

Step Three:

1/4 cup peanut oil
3–4 cloves garlic, minced
1–2" pieces fresh ginger, cut into
   matchsticks
4–6 green onions, sliced diagonally
   into 3/4" pieces
1 Tbsp. dry sherry

Heat wok over medium-high heat until water beads dropped in wok bounce before evaporating. Add oil and swirl to coat wok. Add garlic, ginger, and onions, and stir-fry 1 minute. Add beef and stir-fry 1 minute. Add sherry and continue to stir-fry while sherry sizzles. As soon as sizzling stops, use slotted spoon to remove beef from mixture and place in bowl.

Step Four:

1/2 cup uncooked white rice
1/2 lb. snow peas, cleaned and
   blanched
1 eight-oz. can whole water
   chestnuts, drained
cashews or chopped peanuts

Cook rice according to package directions. Meanwhile, add 1 Tablespoon oil to wok if necessary. Add snow peas and stir-fry 2 minutes. Move snow peas to sides of wok and add well-stirred oyster marinade to wok. As soon as it bubbles, add beef and water chestnuts, and stir until blended. Serve over white rice and garnish with cashews or chopped peanuts if desired.

SUGGESTED MENU

Appeteaser

Bacon-Wrapped Scallops

Less Than Subtle Seduction

Say Yes Salad

Pièce de No Resistance

Wok on the Wild Side

Wine

Sauvignon Blanc

Affaire Nouveau

Your new affair can be as hot as you dare. Let's sizzle tonight!

Beef Filets with Vegetables in Port Wine Cream Sauce

Step One:

1/4 cup port wine
1/2 cup white wine
1 shallot, minced
1/2 cup chicken stock
1 Tbsp. Dijon mustard
1/2 tsp. chervil
1/2 tsp. marjoram
1/2 tsp. tarragon

In small saucepan over medium heat, boil port wine, white wine, and shallot until reduced by half. Stir in stock and reduce by half again. Stir in mustard and herbs, turn heat off, and set aside.

Step Two:

3 cups chicken stock
2 carrots, diagonally sliced into ovals
1 zucchini, diagonally sliced into ovals
3 broccoli florets
4 pearl onions

In large saucepan over medium-high heat, bring stock to a boil. Add carrots, zucchini, and broccoli, and cook until crisp-tender. Use a slotted spoon to remove vegetables to heated bowl. Add onions to saucepan and boil until tender.

Step Three:

2 medium beef filets

Prepare a grill or barbecue and grill filets until cooked to your desire.

Step Four:

1/2 cup whipping cream

Whisk cream into wine sauce and cook over medium heat for 2–3 minutes, or until slightly thickened. Place a filet in the center of each warmed plate. Place vegetables in clusters around beef. Spoon sauce over beef and serve immediately.

SUGGESTED MENU

Appeteaser

Crab and Shrimp Duet

Less Than Subtle Seduction

Are You Game? Greens

Pièce de No Resistance

Affaire Nouveau

Something on the Side

Carrot-Potato Au Gratin

Wine

Pinot Noir

Hot Stuff

1 hour, 20 minutes

She already knows you're hot stuff, but if you play your cards right, you'll get a chance to prove it!

Teriyaki Short Ribs

Step One:

1/2 cup sugar
2/3 cup soy sauce
2 Tbsp. sherry
1 tsp. grated fresh ginger
1 clove garlic, minced
2 Tbsp. oil
2 Tbsp. minced onion
1–1 1/2 lb. boneless beef short
   ribs, well trimmed

Combine ingredients—except ribs—and mix well. Marinate ribs in this sauce for at least 1 hour.

Step Two:

Preheat broiler. Place ribs on broiler pan and broil 3 inches from heat for 4–5 minutes. Turn ribs, brush with marinade, and continue to broil 4–5 minutes longer. Remove ribs to warm serving platter and serve immediately.

SUGGESTED MENU

Appeteaser

Bacon-Wrapped Scallops

Less Than Subtle Seduction

Are You Game? Greens

Pièce de No Resistance

Hot Stuff

Something on the Side

Lemon Rice and Apple Yams

Wine

Gamay Beaujolais

♥Getting Hot Chops

25 minutes

But don't show it, your partner may get cold feet!

Pork Loin Chops in Orange-Ginger Cream Sauce

Step One:

2 boneless pork loin chops
2 tsp. cornstarch
1/4 cup soy sauce
1/3 cup water

Partially freeze pork (meat should not be hard, but firm, with some ice crystals; this process usually takes 30–45 minutes). Slice pork into strips 1/4" thick and 2" long. Blend cornstarch, soy sauce, and water. Add pork and marinate for 15–20 minutes while preparing other ingredients.

Step Two:

1 Tbsp. butter
1 Tbsp. oil
1 Tbsp. minced fresh ginger
1 clove garlic, minced
1 shallot, minced

Heat butter and oil in frying pan over medium-high heat. Add ginger, garlic, and shallot, and stir 30 seconds. Drain pork on paper towels, add to pan, and stir-fry until browned on both sides.

Step Three:

3 Tbsp. grated fresh orange zest
2 Tbsp. sherry
3/4 cup whipping cream
1/2 cup mandarin orange sections
1 Tbsp. snipped fresh chives

Whisk orange zest and sherry into pan and cook 30 seconds. Add cream and simmer, stirring frequently, until slightly thickened. Add mandarin oranges just before serving and stir gently to warm through. Spoon mixture into warm au gratin dishes, sprinkle with chives, and serve immediately.

Appeteaser

Bacon-Wrapped Scallops

Less Than Subtle Seduction

Say Yes Salad

Pièce de No Resistance

♥*Getting Hot Chops*

Something on the Side

Lemon Rice and Pistachio Carrots

Wine

Chenin Blanc

Papaya Passions

Don't play under the papaya tree with anyone else but me!

Pork Nuggets with Papaya and Cashews

Step One:

1/2 cup flour
1/4 cup water
1 egg, beaten
1 tsp. salt
1 lb. boneless pork loin, cubed and
   patted dry
peanut oil

Mix flour, water, egg, and salt in bowl. Add pork cubes and toss until well coated. In a large frying pan over medium-high heat, heat oil and add pork in batches, frying until golden brown on all sides. Remove pork to paper towels to drain.

Step Two:

1 cup uncooked white rice
1/4 cup red wine vinegar
1/2 cup water
2 Tbsp. brown sugar
1/4 cup pineapple juice
1 Tbsp. cornstarch
1/2 papaya, peeled, seeded, and cut
   into bite-size cubes
1/2 cup cashews
1 Tbsp. chopped fresh parsley

Cook rice according to package directions. In small saucepan over medium heat, combine vinegar, water, and brown sugar. Bring to a boil, stirring frequently. In a small bowl, blend pineapple juice and cornstarch well; stir into vinegar and cook, stirring frequently, until thickened. Gently fold in pork, papaya, and cashews. Serve on a bed of white rice. Garnish with chopped parsley.

Appeteaser

Gratin of Crab

Less Than Subtle Seduction

Hanky Panky Greens

Pièce de No Resistance

♥Papaya Passions

Something on the Side

Apple Yams

Wine

Riesling

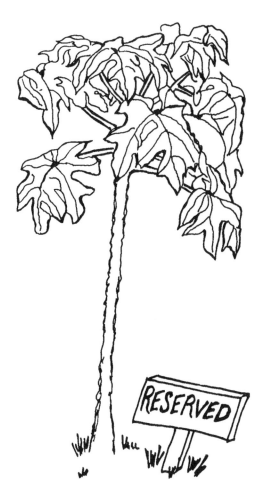

♥ Magic Moments

. . . could be yours tonight if you get your lover to treat you right!

Noisettes of Lamb in Roquefort Sauce

Step One:

2 pieces sourdough or wheat bread,
  crusts removed
3 Tbsp. butter, softened

Preheat oven to 350° F. Butter both sides of bread and place on baking sheet. Bake for 7–10 minutes or until golden brown. Place in warmed au gratin dishes.

Step Two:

1 Tbsp. butter
1 clove garlic, minced
5 oz. frozen chopped spinach,
  thawed and drained

Melt butter in frying pan. Sauté garlic and spinach over low heat while completing next step.

Step Three:

1 Tbsp. butter
2 lamb noisettes, cut 1 1/4" thick
  (have butcher prepare them for you)

Melt butter in second frying pan over medium heat. Add lamb and cook, turning once, 5–6 minutes per side. Remove lamb to warmed plate.

Step Four:

1 clove garlic, minced
1 tsp. capers, rinsed and mashed
1/2 cup port wine
1/3 cup whipping cream
1/3 cup Roquefort or bleu cheese
parsley sprigs

Pour off pan drippings, add garlic, capers, and port to pan. Boil over high heat until reduced to about 1/4 cup. Whisk in cream and cook until reduced by half. Whisk in cheese until melted. To assemble, top bread rounds with spinach, then lamb, nap with sauce, and garnish with parsley.

SUGGESTED MENU

Appeteaser

Crab and Shrimp Duet

Less Than Subtle Seduction

Are You Game? Greens

Pièce de No Resistance

♥ Magic Moments

Something on the Side

Vegetable Sauté

Wine

Merlot

 *Flashin' Passion*

Will you still love me tomorrow?

Noisettes of Lamb in Pecan Sauce

Step One:

3 Tbsp. toasted and chopped
   pecans
3 Tbsp. butter
2 Tbsp. minced onions
1 Tbsp. minced mushrooms
3–4 Tbsp. rich lamb or beef stock

In food processor, blend pecans, butter, onions, and mushrooms for 1 minute. Scrape down sides of bowl and add enough stock to make a paste. Blend until paste is of uniform consistency.

Step Two:

1/2 cup rich lamb or beef stock
3 Tbsp. red wine vinegar
2 Tbsp. port wine
1/4 cup minced leek
1 Tbsp. minced onion
2 Tbsp. minced mushrooms
1/3 cup whipping cream
2 Tbsp. butter
dash of Tabasco sauce
2 tsp. bourbon

In large saucepan, combine stock, vinegar, wine, leek, onion, and mushrooms and bring to a boil. Continue boiling until liquid is reduced to 2 Tablespoons. Add cream and continue to boil until thickened. Turn off heat and whisk in butter. Stir in paste from Step One, then stir in Tabasco sauce and bourbon. Remove from heat and set the saucepan in a pan of hot water to keep it warm.

Step Three:

4–6 lamb loin chops, well
   trimmed of fat
corn oil or light olive oil
salt and pepper to taste
4–6 pecan halves, toasted
2 small clusters of red grapes

Grease rack of barbecue or grill and adjust for medium-high heat. Bone each lamb chop, tying meat from each chop into a small bundle with cotton string. Rub chops with oil and season with salt and pepper. Grill chops 4–7 minutes per side for medium rare meat. For rarer or more well done meat, adjust cooking time accordingly. Spoon sauce into warmed au gratin dishes, top with lamb bundles, and garnish with pecan halves and red grape clusters. Serve.

SUGGESTED MENU

Appeteaser

Gratin of Crab

Less Than Subtle Seduction

Say Yes Salad

Pièce de No Resistance

Flashin' Passion

Something on the Side

Lemon Rice and Apple Yams

Wine

Pinot Noir

Fun and Game Hens

1 hour, 40 minutes

It's how you play the game that counts.

Walnut-Stuffed Game Hens in Black Currant Sauce

Step One:

2 slices bacon
1/4 cup minced onion
1/3 cup chopped mushrooms
1 cup dried coarse bread crumbs
1/3 cup chopped walnuts
salt to taste
1/4 tsp. thyme
1/4 tsp. sage
2 game hens

Fry bacon until crisp. Remove bacon from pan, reserve drippings, and drain bacon on paper towels. Over medium heat, sauté onion and mushrooms in bacon drippings until tender. Remove and combine with remaining ingredients, tossing lightly. Stuff hens with walnut stuffing and close openings with wooden toothpicks.

Step Two:

3 Tbsp. butter
2 Tbsp. dry white wine
1/4 tsp. garlic, minced
1/8 tsp. sage

Preheat oven to 400° F. Melt butter in small pan, add remaining ingredients, and mix well. Place hens breast side up in roasting pan. Brush hens with basting sauce. Roast 1 hour, basting occasionally. Remove hens to warm serving platter. Cover loosely and keep warm.

Step Three:

1 Tbsp. flour
1/4 cup dry white wine
1/4 cup black currant jelly
1/4 tsp. dry mustard
salt to taste

Pour off all but 2/3 cup drippings from roasting pan. Place pan on stovetop over medium heat; whisk in flour until smooth. Cook 2 minutes. Add remaining ingredients and bring to a boil; reduce heat and simmer until thickened. Pour sauce into serving boat and pass.

SUGGESTED MENU

Appeteaser

Sautéed Camembert

Less Than Subtle Seduction

Sweet Potato Soup

Pièce de No Resistance

Fun and Game Hens

Something on the Side

Vegetable Sauté

Wine

Fumé Blanc

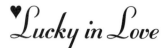
♥ Lucky in Love

1 hour, 20 minutes

Double your pleasure in the game of love.

Spiced Cornish Game Hens with Mandarin Oranges

Step One:

1 cup dry white wine
1/4 cup plus 2 Tbsp. soy sauce
1/4 cup butter
2 Tbsp. flour
reserved juice from one 11-oz. can
   mandarin oranges
1 tsp. grated fresh lime zest
2 Tbsp. lemon juice
1 tsp. oregano
1 tsp. thyme
1 tsp. ginger
1 tsp. curry powder
1 tsp. honey

Preheat oven to 400° F. In a saucepan over medium heat, combine wine and soy sauce and bring to a simmer. In a second saucepan over low heat, melt butter, whisk in flour, and cook 7 minutes. Remove from heat and whisk in wine mixture and mandarin orange juice. Cook over medium heat until thickened. Remove from heat. Add remaining ingredients and whisk until thoroughly blended.

Step Two:

2 Cornish game hens, halved
1 eleven-oz. can mandarin oranges,
   drained and juice reserved
parsley sprigs

Arrange hens, skin side up, in large baking pan. Spoon sauce over hens and bake 50 minutes, basting occasionally. During last 15 minutes, add orange sections to pan drippings and heat through. Place hens on warm platter, garnish with oranges and parsley sprigs, and serve.

Appeteaser

Stuffed Grape Leaves

Less Than Subtle Seduction

Hanky Panky Greens

Pièce de No Resistance

♥*Lucky in Love*

Something on the Side

Apple Yams

Wine

Fumé Blanc

♥ Lusty Lapin

Rabbits have a habit,
you will too,
we all know what rabbits do!

Rabbit in Port Wine-Grape Sauce

Step One:

2 Tbsp. butter
1 Tbsp. oil
1 clove garlic, minced
1/2 rabbit, cut into serving pieces
salt and pepper to taste

Melt butter and oil in large frying pan over medium-low heat. Add garlic to pan and sauté until golden. Season rabbit with salt and pepper. Add rabbit to pan and sauté until browned on both sides.

Step Two:

1 cup seedless red flame grapes
1/2 cup port wine
1/2 cup chicken stock
2 Tbsp. minced leek

Combine grapes, wine, stock, and leek in small saucepan over medium heat and bring to a boil. Reduce heat and simmer for 2 minutes. Remove grapes, turn heat to high, and boil sauce until reduced by half.

Step Three:

2 Tbsp. butter
1 tsp. cornstarch
1 tsp. tarragon vinegar
2 tsp. port wine
salt and pepper to taste

Blend butter and cornstarch. Add this mixture, 1 Tablespoon at a time, to sauce, blending well. Boil sauce for 1 minute, then add vinegar and wine. Season with salt and pepper. (If sauce is too thick, use a little stock to thin it.) Lay rabbit in warmed au gratin dishes and spoon sauce over it. Serve immediately.

SUGGESTED MENU

Appeteaser

Stuffed Grape Leaves

Less Than Subtle Seduction

Are You Game? Greens

Pièce de No Resistance

♥*Lusty Lapin*

Something on the Side

Artichoke Fromage

Wine

Merlot

(Vegetables)

Artichoke Fromage

40 minutes

Step One:

2 Tbsp. butter
1/2 onion, sliced
1 leek, chopped
6 mushrooms, sliced
1 eight-oz. jar marinated artichoke
   hearts, drained and quartered
3 cloves garlic, minced
1 Tbsp. chopped fresh parsley
1 Tbsp. chopped fresh basil
1/4 tsp. freshly ground pepper

Preheat oven to 350° F. Butter shallow baking dish or quiche dish. Melt 2 Tablespoons butter in frying pan over medium heat. Add onion, leek, and mushrooms, and sauté until soft. Add artichokes, garlic, parsley, basil, and pepper. Cook 5 minutes. Pour mixture into baking dish.

Step Two:

1/4 cup mayonnaise
1/4 cup sour cream
2 Tbsp. whipping cream
1 Tbsp. hot mustard
1/4 cup fresh, coarse bread crumbs
1/4 cup Parmesan

Blend mayonnaise, sour cream, whipping cream, and mustard thoroughly in bowl. Spread mixture evenly over artichoke mixture. Mix bread crumbs with Parmesan cheese. Sprinkle over mayonnaise mixture and bake 25 minutes or until golden brown.

Pistachio Carrots

10 minutes

Step One:

8–10 baby carrots, tops removed

Steam carrots until just crisp-tender.

Step Two:

2 Tbsp. butter
1/2 cup shelled pistachios
2 Tbsp. Triple Sec

Melt butter in small saucepan over medium heat. Add pistachios and sauté 1–2 minutes. Stir in Triple Sec and remove from heat. Add carrots and toss gently, coating carrots with sauce. Serve immediately.

Apple Yams

Step One:

1 yam

Add yam to boiling water, cover and cook 30 minutes, or until tender. Cool slightly, remove skin, and cut into slices 1/4" or less in thickness.

Step Two:

1 large Granny Smith apple,
  thinly sliced
cinnamon
3–4 Tbsp. brown sugar
1/4 cup butter, melted
3 tsp. brandy

Preheat oven to 350° F. Grease a 9" quiche or pie pan. Arrange a layer of alternating yam and apple slices on the bottom of the pan. Sprinkle with a layer of cinnamon and brown sugar, and drizzle with butter. Add another layer of apples and yams, sprinkle with cinnamon and brown sugar, and drizzle with butter. Repeat layers until all ingredients have been used. Bake, covered, 30 minutes. Remove cover and continue to bake 40 minutes longer. Sprinkle with brandy just prior to serving.

Carrot-Potato Au Gratin

25 minutes

Step One:

2 carrots, peeled and quartered
2 medium red potatoes, peeled
  and quartered

Steam or boil potatoes and carrots until tender.

Step Two:

1 egg
1/4 cup grated Parmesan cheese
1 Tbsp. butter
1 Tbsp. sour cream
1/4 tsp. dry mustard
pinch of cayenne
1/2 Tbsp. butter

Preheat broiler. Butter a small baking dish or individual ramekins. Mash potatoes and carrots. Add egg, 3 Tablespoons of the Parmesan, butter, sour cream, mustard, and cayenne. Purée using mixer or food processor. Spoon into baking dish or ramekins, sprinkle with remaining Parmesan, and dot with butter. Broil 2–3 minutes or until golden brown. Serve.

Vegetable Sauté

Step One:

1 small zucchini, cut into 1" pieces
2 carrots, cut into 1" pieces
6 Brussels sprouts

Steam vegetables until crisp-tender. Cover loosely and keep warm.

Step Two:

1 Tbsp. butter
1 Tbsp olive oil
6 cherry tomatoes
1 Tbsp. minced fresh parsley
1/2 tsp. basil
1/2 tsp. marjoram
1/2 tsp. chervil
2 Tbsp. lime juice
2 Tbsp. Parmesan

In small frying pan, melt butter and oil over medium heat and sauté tomatoes and herbs for 2 minutes. Turn heat off and stir in lime juice. Put vegetables in warm serving bowl, and pour sauce over them. Sprinkle with Parmesan and toss gently. Serve immediately.

Lemon Rice

25 minutes

1/2 cup uncooked white rice
1 egg
2 Tbsp. fresh lemon juice
2 Tbsp. freshly grated Parmesan cheese
2 Tbsp. minced fresh parsley
salt and pepper to taste

Cook rice according to package directions. Just before serving, combine egg, lemon juice, Parmesan, and parsley in bowl and mix well. Season with salt and pepper. Stir mixture into hot rice and blend well.

SUBJECT INDEX

RECIPE INDEX

NAUGHTY NOTES
(Notes)

NAUGHTY NOTES

(Notes)

NAUGHTY NOTES
(Notes)

NAUGHTY NOTES
(Notes)

NAUGHTY NOTES

(Notes)

NAUGHTY NOTES

(Notes)